RIVER TAILS

BRYAN ROBINSON

To order additional copies of this book, contact:
Xlibris
844-714-8691
www.Xlibris.com
Orders@Xlibris.com

ISBN: Softcover   978-1-6641-2740-1
            EBook   978-1-6641-2883-5

Print information available on the last page

Rev. date: 09/03/2020

Bryan Robinson has written and edited for many people, and they all have supported him doing the same. Wally Madding of Montana, Antonio Solis of XLibris, his deceased wife Bren, Ann McCollum of Montana, his sister Raejeanne of Texas, Carol of Washington, Charmaine of Washington, readers of his "Funny Farm" "blog" all over the U.S.; and his new partner Pat of Colbert, WA, and her daughter Sandra have contributed greatly.

Pat is also a photographer, and has 6 computers, scanners, big printers, and knew how to take an old, yellowed photo given to Bryan by the Forest Service of him rafting down the Rogue River, and reproduce it for the cover. She has encouraged me to resume my photography and writing and now accompanies me all over Eastern Washington photographing many things of interest for many future books, underway. And I am having fun again.

Every summer we floated down many rivers, like the Columbia, Snake, Rio Grande, Colorado, Yakima, and others, but did I ever tell you about the time I was floating down the Rogue River in the mid 1970's?

Where the huge Rogue River begins up high with a trickle

We had made a raft out of purple Popsicle sticks, and grabbed onto the tails of huge salmon who turned around and headed back downstream, helping us go straight down the current rather than bumping into the rocks. Each time he, or we got tired, we would let go and pull over to the sandy shore and eat, or camp for the night.

We wrestled bears and ate them, along with the berries we picked. We washed off all the bear grease and berry juice and showered, under the waterfalls. The water would come down on us so hard it would push our hair down and form a hat to protect us from the sun.

Waterfalls also feed the river

We would carve new oars to replace the ones we broke whacking the bears over the heads. We cut vines to loop around the oars to hold them in place as we rowed.

Sometimes, salmon that didn't like to have their tails held, would simply get under the raft in pairs and lift us slightly out of the water and glide us along our way.

We would grab small fish, for us to eat, out of the mouths of the great blue herons and pelicans as we floated by them. They would get so mad. They would make croaking noises, and usually fly overhead, depositing the fish they had eaten the previous day, right on our heads. We smelled really bad, and had slick skin, at the end of each day.

Swallows build their mud nests against the rocks

We hated the people who littered trash, but we would do our part in cleaning up by taking coke bottles and breaking them so we could use the bottoms for sunglasses. After a couple of days we looked like raccoons because our faces were red from the water reflection, yet our eyes were white. Male raccoons along the shores became a real nuisance because they thought we were pretty.

Water shapes contours into rocks

I hated the water snakes, but would collect them so I could tie my sleeping bag up between two trees like a hammock, because I hated the insects worse.

I remember watching a scorpion, who could not swim, asking a frog to help him get to the other side of the river and the frog said he would not transport him because he was afraid the scorpion would sting him. The scorpion kept promising the frog he would not sting him, so the frog finally gave in and told the scorpion to get on his back.

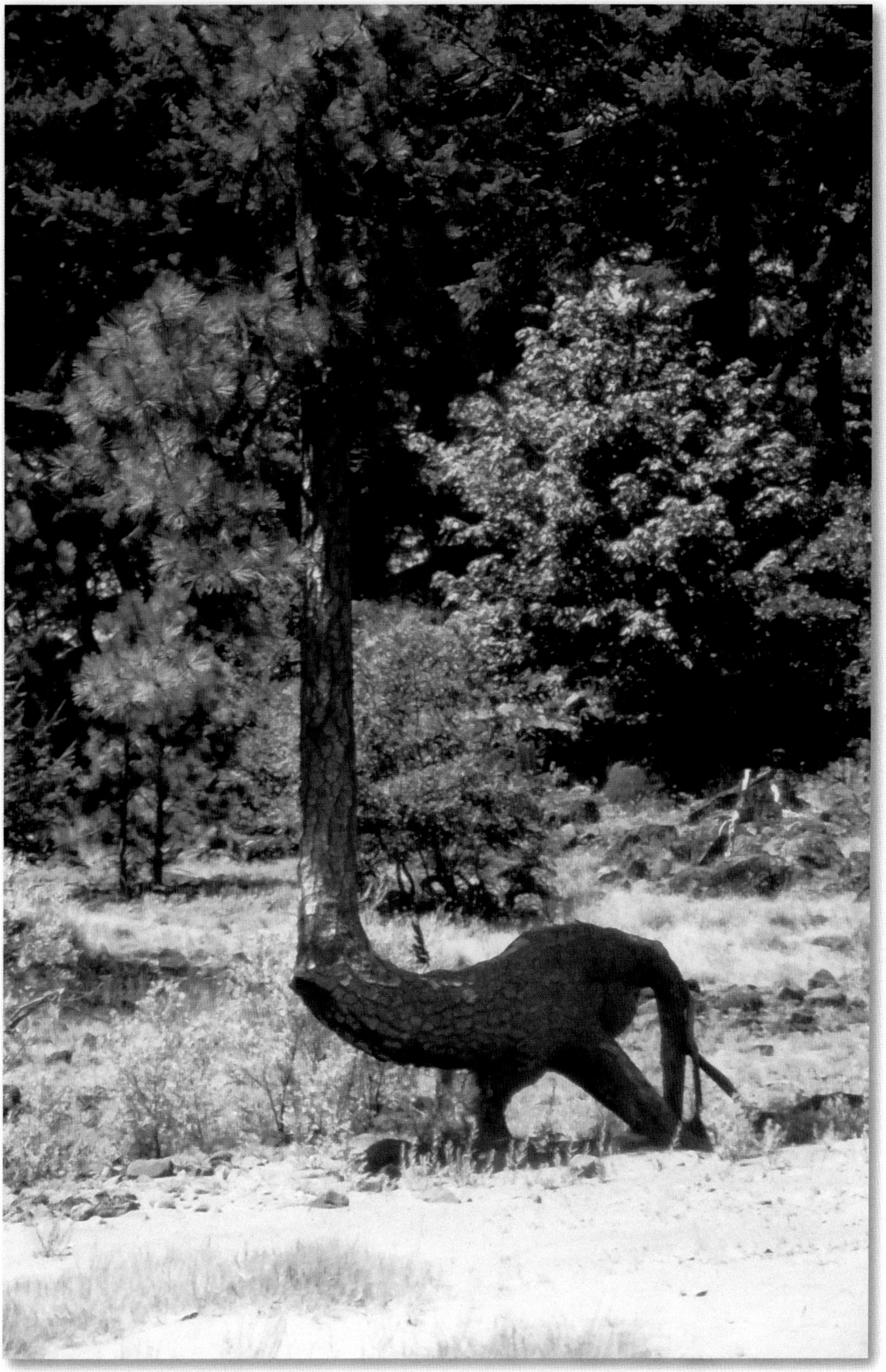

Some tree trunks look like animals

The frog kicked his legs and got the scorpion across the worst part of the river and was almost to the other side, when sure enough, the scorpion raised his stinger and stuck the frog. Just before the frog collapsed and drowned at the shore, I heard him say to the scorpion "Why did you do that? I thought you promised not to sting me. I trusted you, and now I'm going to die after doing you a favor." I watched the scorpion smile and heard him say "I'm sorry, but I'm a scorpion and that's what I do. I don't know how to do anything else but sting." We all have friends like that, that want us to drown, and must be careful of them.

The thrill and dunking of rafting over rough waters

I was still thinking about the frog when we set up our next camp. We had caught a bunch of crawdads in the creek and the new people thought they were lobsters. We also caught some frogs and were preparing a lobster and frog leg dinner. We were putting some of them in the hot, boiling pot, and they would try to get out. The crawdads couldn't get out, but it was not easy to keep the jumping frogs in the pot. We figured out that if we put them in the pot of water while it was still cool, neither the crawdads or the frogs would try to get out. That was because they only had a gradual change, one degree at a time, until it was so hot they had no strength to get out.

Author resting and cooling off in side-waters

That's the same way it is with people. They let their friends influence them and let things happen to them in little steps, so they don't notice it. Anything or anybody would get out of a boiling pot. But if it sneaks up on us one step at a time, we don't notice it until it is too late. It's better not to ever get in the pot in the first place. Even if it feels warm and fuzzy at the beginning. Better yet, it is better to be like the frogs and crawdads that never let us catch them in the first place. Once they are in the pot, neither their friends nor their parents can help them anymore.

Tame deer watching camp cook

Another thing we did in camp was to play tic- tac-toe in the sand. I loved that game because the whole time I would be thinking about a book I had read a long time ago, which made me feel better about when others weren't nice to me. The book was about X's and O's. It showed pictures of many X's, representing most people, like:

XXXXXXXXXXXXXXXXXXXXXXXXXXXXXXXXXXX
XXXXXXXXXXXXXXXXXXXXXXXXXXXXXXXXXXX
XXXXXXXXXXXXXXXXXXXXXXXXXXXXXXXXXXX
XXXXXXXXXXXXXXXXXXXXXXXXXXXXXXXXXXX
XXXXXXXXXXXXXXXXXXXXXXXXXXXXXXXXXXX
XXXXXXXXXXXXXXXXXXX

These people lie, and cheat, and steal, and hit their brothers and sisters, and are rude to their parents, and cause trouble in school, and do things they shouldn't do after school. They are spoiled and do not appreciate their homes or food or clothing, or parents who give them rules to guide them to a good life and to keep them safe.

Then just one **O** is added, representing **YOU,** who is different and feeling lost in the middle somewhere, like:

XXXXXXXXXXXXXXXXXXXXXXXXXXXXXXXXXXXX

XXXXXXXXXXXXXXXXXXXXXXXXXXXXXXXXXXXX

XXXXXXXXXXXXXXXXXXXXXXXXXXXXXXXXXXXX

XXXXXX**O**XXXXXXXXXXXXXXXXXXXXXXXXXXXXX XXX

XXXXXXXXXXXXXXXXXXXXXXXXXXXXXXXXXXXX

XXXXXXXXXXXXXXXXXXXXXXXXXXXXXXXXXXXXX

You would and could not, and should not try, to ever become like the others no matter how much they try to influence you, and if you stay true to yourself, eventually it would be like:

And then it would eventually be like this:

XXXXXXXXXXXXXXXXXXXXXXXXXXXXXXXXXXXX
XXXXXXXXXXXXXXXXXXXXXXXXXXXXXXXXXXXX
XXXXXXXXXXXXXXXXXXXXXXXXXXXXXXXXXXXX
XXXXOOXXXXXXXXXXXXXXXXXXXXXXXXXXXXXX
XXXXXXXXXXXXXXXXXXXXXXXXXXXXXXXXX XXX
XXXXXXXXXXXXXXXXXXXXXXXXXXXXXXXXXXXX
XXXXXXXXX

And later like:

OXXXXXXXXXXXXXXXXXXXXXXXXXXXXXXXXXXOXXX
X XXXXXXXXXXXXXXXXXXXXXXXXXXXXXXXXXXXXX
XXXXXXXXXXXXXXXXXXXXXXXXXXXXXXXXXXXXXX
XX**O**OXXXXXXXXXXXXXXXXXXXXXXXXXXXXXXXX
XXXXXXXXXXXXXXXXXXXXXXXXXXXXXXXXXXXXXX
XXXXXXXXXXXXXXXOXXXXXXXXXXXXXXXXXXXXXX
XXXXXXXXXO

And if you hang on to who you really are and what you know is right, even more will join you like:

OXXXXOXXXXXXXXXXXXXXOXXXXXXXOX
XXXXXXXXXXXXXXOXXXXXXXXXXXXXXX
XXOXXXXXXXXXXXXXXXOXXXXXXXXXXX
XXXXXXXXXXXOOOOOXXXXXXXXXXXXXX
XXOXXXXXXXXXXXXXXXXXOXXXXXXXXX
XXXXXXXXXXXXXOXXXXXXXXXXXXXXOXXX
XXXXOXXXXXXXXXXXXXXXXXXOO

But there will always be the majority of X's, trying to make you be just like them, and do things just like them, that deep inside you know are not right and not like you.

You are special, and you cannot ever let others make you think you are not.

And **you know what is right**.

And **you know the difference** between what makes you feel good for a short time as compared to what makes you feel good for a long time.

And **you know what makes you feel proud** of yourself and what makes your parents proud of you.

And **you know it is your very own choice** that makes you stay yourself, or become like the other X's that look exciting and like they are having such a good time at first.

Another riverside camp visito

But **since you will stand alone for a while**, and watch, you will end up happy, and you will see the other X's get into trouble and end up unhappy. But you must remember while they are drowning, they will appear to not be drowning, and will laugh and pretend, and try to get you to cross over to their side, so they can walk away like the scorpions, and leave you like the frog to drown.

Or you can have real fun floating on the many wonderful rivers of life. It's your choice. And they are simple choices, because **you already know**.

The author with steelhead. The Rogue River is famous for big steelhead and salmon. (One stop is at the famous author Zane Grey's cabin. He wrote Rogue River Feud)."

Printed in the United States
by Baker & Taylor Publisher Services